THE KLUTZ BOOK OF ANIMATION

by John Cassidy and Nicholas Berger

KLUTZ

A TWO-PART TABLE OF CONTENTS

The Book

The Klutz Book of Animation (the book, the thing you're holding in your hands right now) is one-half of a multimedia presentation. It's the instructional part, the backstage tour. It contains all the secrets, tricks, and techniques that you'll need to make the animated videos that you'll find at Klutz.com/ani.

The Videos

The videos that you'll be learning how to make are all online. You need to watch them before you start, even if you only use them to jump off to your own ideas. To see them, go to klutz.com/ani.

<u>KLUTZ.com/ani</u>
Check them out!

NOW SHOWING

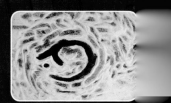

The Most Popular Magic Trick of All Time

I'm alive!

In the real world, things are sort of boring: Chairs don't walk, brooms don't fly, mice don't talk, and little clay characters don't have fun adventures.

But in the world of animation, things are very different.

Animation is an optical trick that relies on the fact that our eye/brain connection can only do so much. If you were watching an ordinary slide show, and then dialed up the speed until the pictures were running fast enough, they would start to blur together. Call it the brain's speed limit. Somewhere around 10 fps (frames per second) the gaps between the pictures disappear and the picture starts to "move" (making "movies").

About 150 years ago, a couple of people figured out the trick of animation could be used to create some moving picture toys, unpronounceably called "thaumatropes," "zoetropes," and "phenakistoscopes." Check out page 63 for a ratty version of a phenakistoscope that you can punch out and use.

ILLUSIONS

Thaumatrope, the beginnings of animation

Phenakistoscope (See page 63.)

CLAYMATION

How to make lumps of clay sing and dance.

How to make paper dolls fly through outer space.

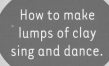

CUT-OUT ANIMATION

How to make eggs scurry around the house.

How to make a photograph go for a walk.

Isn't Animation Just a Fancy Word for Cart**oo**ning?

Cartooning (where a series of drawings is made to come alive) is just one flavor of animation. Thanks to Mickey Mouse and Bart Simpson, people tend to think it's the only one. But "traditional cell animation" (as it's technically called) is just the most common style; there are many more. For example, in this book, we're going to be doing...

OBJECT ANIMATION

PHOTO ANIMATION

How to make people move in magical ways.

How to make animation speed up snails.

PIXILATION

TIME LAPSE

How to turn video into animation.

ROTOSCOPING

THE TRICKINESS SCALE: Some of the animations we've described in this book take less than an hour to do. And some of them can take most of the day. We recommend you start with the simplest and work up. Look for these symbols.

DIFFICULTY LEVEL **1** Easy   DIFFICULTY LEVEL **2** Medium   DIFFICULTY LEVEL **3** Tricky

5

The Three Steps of Animation

1 **Take a picture of something.**

2 **Change it.**

3 **Shoot it again.**

Regardless of the technique used, or the thing drawn or photographed, animation can always be boiled down to three steps:

1 Take a still picture of something (a drawing, a banana, a guy on the lawn...).

2 Change it a little bit.

3 Shoot it again.

Repeat.

When you run all the little still pictures together in front of your eyes very quickly, the magic appears: The banana sings, the guy flies, the drawing runs around.

How to perform these miracles is what the rest of this book is about.

Any kind of computer works.

What Do I Need to Start?

A computer. As long as it isn't ancient (like 10 years old) it doesn't matter what kind, PC or Mac.

A video camera. Doesn't matter if it's just a $20 webcam or the basic video camera you can get at the drugstore. Pretty much anything works.

Any kind of video camera

The Connection

The cable. The camera has to be attached to the computer when you shoot. That's why you'll be working indoors (unless you have a laptop you can take outside). Most webcams and video cameras come with cables meant to connect them to your computer. Go find yours, you'll need it.

Once your camera is plugged into your computer, and you've put the star of your show in front of your camera, you're ready to put the software into your computer.

Download Animation Software

Meet SAM. If you have your own animation software preloaded on your computer, and you know how to use it, you're all set. If you don't, the animation software we used and recommend is called the SAM Animation Program and we'll show you where to get it at **klutz.com/ani**. It's a free download, and it runs on either Windows or Mac and is incredibly easy to use. It was developed by the Tufts University Center for Engineering Education and Outreach specifically for "which-end-of-the-camera-do-I-hold?" beginners.

This is what your
camera is staring at.

Getting to Know the Software

Your Work Screen

If you're using SAM, you should be looking at this screen after you've done all the start-up stuff. On the screen should be a picture of whatever your camera is staring at. **✱**

This is your work screen and it's where you'll be living as you make your movie. There are two buttons that you really need to know.

Playback
Click on this to play your movie.

Snap picture
Click on this to take your pictures.

Nothing here.
Bad sign.

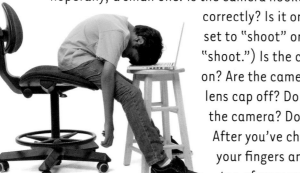

✱ What if I don't see anything? Then you have a problem — hopefully, a small one. Is the camera hooked up to the computer correctly? Is it on? Do you have the camera set to "shoot" or "playback"? (Better be "shoot.") Is the computer plugged in and on? Are the camera's batteries good? Is the lens cap off? Do you have anything in front of the camera? Double-check the connection. After you've checked your connections, cross your fingers and go to the **camera** menu at the top of your screen and select **refresh camera**.

What about all the other buttons on the work screen?

You can add sound and do all sorts of editing tricks with the other buttons on the screen. We'll be talking about these buttons later in the book, but for now there are two ways to learn the basics about them:

• **Experiment.** Play around. Use your new film to test-drive the buttons.

• **Look at the video tutorial.** We'll show you where to find it at **klutz.com/ani**.

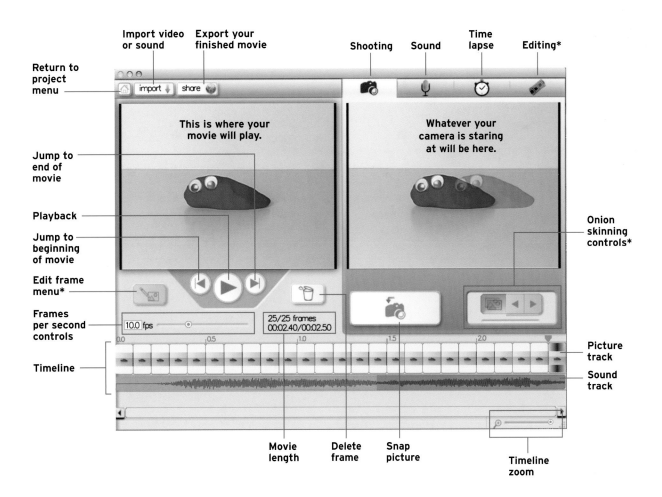

Import video or sound

Export your finished movie

Shooting

Sound

Time lapse

Editing*

Return to project menu

This is where your movie will play.

Whatever your camera is staring at will be here.

Jump to end of movie

Playback

Jump to beginning of movie

Edit frame menu*

Frames per second controls

10.0 fps

25/25 frames
00:02.40/00:02.50

Timeline

Onion skinning controls*

Picture track

Sound track

Movie length

Delete frame

Snap picture

Timeline zoom

* Disabled in free version of SAM

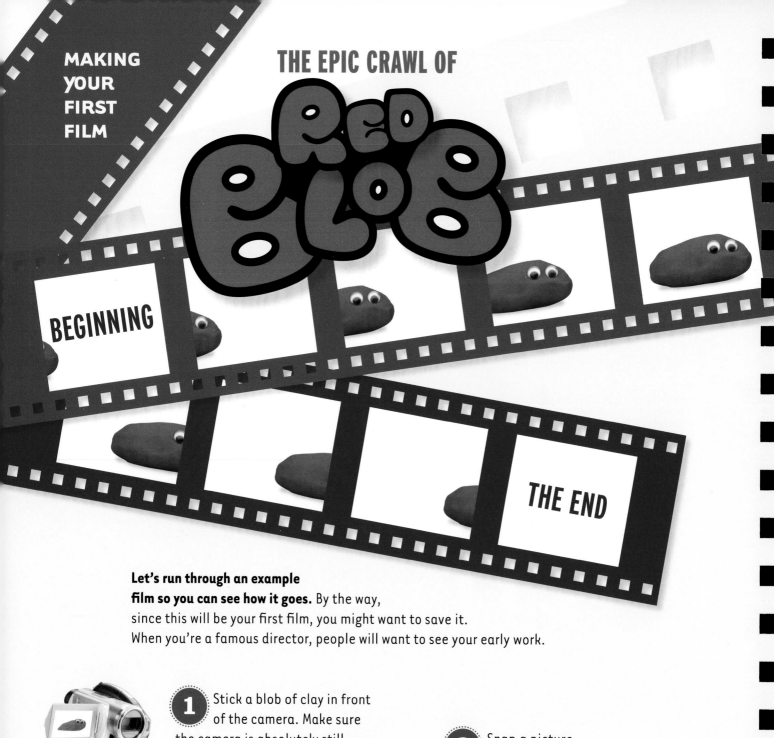

THE EPIC CRAWL OF RED BLOB

BEGINNING

THE END

Let's run through an example film so you can see how it goes. By the way, since this will be your first film, you might want to save it. When you're a famous director, people will want to see your early work.

1 Stick a blob of clay in front of the camera. Make sure the camera is absolutely still. You'll want to use a tripod or put it on a table.

2 Snap a picture. (Either hit the space bar, like we do, or click the **snap picture ▶ button** on your screen.)

3 Move the clay just a tad.

4 Snap another picture. ▼

5 Go ahead and click the **playback ▶ button** right now. How's your movie look so far? (Answer? Short.)

Here are the two screens you just used.

AFTER taking the first picture and getting ready to take the second

BEFORE taking the first picture

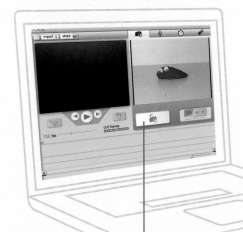

To take a picture, hit the space bar or click here. Your choice.

To lengthen your movie, move the clay another tad and snap another picture. You'll notice, by the way, that there are ghosts on the screen. Every time you move the clay, you'll see a "ghost" of where it used to be. This is called an "onion skin" of the old image and it's there to help you line up your new movement and keep the action smooth. Extremely helpful.

To finish your movie, repeat: Shoot, move, shoot, move, shoot, move... After a while, stop and push the playback button. Your first film! Congratulations!

THE END!

Onion skin. This is a ghost of the first picture you took. It hangs around to let you position the new picture.

This is the new picture you're getting ready to take.

Tips and Tricks

1 Focus on the movement. Don't spend a lot of time constructing elaborate backgrounds or characters. Keep the backgrounds clean and simple so you can focus on the magic of animation — the movement of it.

2 Pick the right animation technique for your story. If your star likes to do a lot of morphing, try claymation. If your star wants to be you (or some other real person), try pixilation — or cut-outs and photos. If you want to make your doodles come to life, think about cartooning.

In other words, match the technique to your story.

3 Speed. How fast (and how smoothly) your character moves depends on how much you move it between shots — that's your pedal and you should push it more or less depending on what's going on in your story. Note: Don't get carried away. Things can look a little jerky if you move too much between shots.

4 Playback speed. SAM animation lets you adjust how quickly your animation plays back, measured in frames per second (fps). The standard playback rate is 10 fps and that's where the program is set automatically; but it's a dial you can adjust. Moving it up means the motion will be smoother, but you'll need to take more pictures. Moving it down means fewer pictures, but choppier motion. It's up to you.

5 Keep looking back. As you shoot, check your progress by hitting the playback button frequently. If you've made mistakes... there's always that delete button. Use it frame by frame.

Sound Effects

Animation without a sound track is like a song without the music — you get the idea but it's only half the show. When things fall down, fly away, slide on the ice, break the window, explode into atoms or just drop into a chair... you'll need the right bop, splat, ping, crunch, or bang to make it come alive.

Here are the two main ways to get sounds and music into your animation.

❶ Record it yourself. You can bang your own pots and pans or record your own blood-curdling screams by using the microphone built into your computer.

Just click on the **sound tab** and then press the **record button**. Once you've recorded your sounds or music, it shows up on your timeline as an **audio track** and you can move it around to the right spot using your mouse.

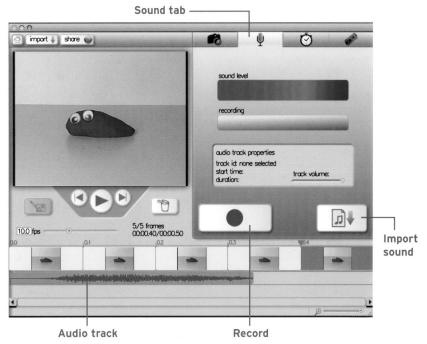

Sound tab

sound level

recording

audio track properties
track id: none selected
start time:
duration: track volume:

10.0 fps   5/5 frames
                        00:00.40/00:00.50

Import sound

Audio track   Record

❷ Import the sound. SAM allows you to import sound effects or music that you have on your computer. We recorded 12 classic sounds for you that will be useful making the projects in this book. We'll show you where to find them at **klutz.com/ani**. You can also import audio files if you have your own collection. And then, of course, there's the web: Try a Google search for free libraries of music or sound effects. No matter where you get them, when you're ready to import a sound file, just click on the **import sound button**.

Model Car
Smashups

SCRIPT: Toy cars race around the room, smash into each other, fly off the tabletop, crash some more. The end.

INGREDIENTS: Two toy cars and some tape.

DIFFICULTY LEVEL
1

❶ Shoot.

❷ Move the cars a tad.

❸ Shoot again.

To animate a car race, follow the basic rule of animation: Move, shoot, move, shoot, move, shoot, move, shoot, move, shoot, move, shoot, and repeat.

Go watch it.
www.klutz.com/ani

How do I make the cars look like they're going faster?

Move them more between shots. The more you move them, the faster they look. Caution: If you move them too far, the motion gets jerky.

Slow

Scoot the car just a hair between shots.

Fast

Scoot the car a lot farther between shots.

How do I make the cars look like they're falling?

Use invisible tape to attach the cars to the wall. This makes them look like they're in mid-air, and it works a lot better than you might think. The tape disappears because of the movement.

The secret

The car reaches the end of the shelf and...

Tape the car to the wall. Shoot. Move.

Tape the car to the wall. Shoot. Move.

!.Kerpow!

15

Choose your angles

Shoot from more than one angle to add excitement to the scene. Here are the three basics.

Shooting from profile

Shooting from the front

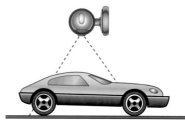

Shooting overhead

What's a tracking shot?

When the camera moves along with the target, that's called a tracking shot. Here the camera is moving along with the cars, but the angle is always profile.

How do I make sure the cars are lined up with the camera perfectly?

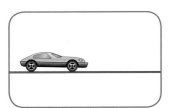

Before you shoot...

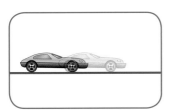

...scoot the camera and line the car up...

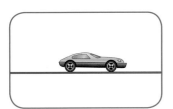

...with the "old" car that's been onion-skinned. Ready to shoot.

How to Do a Tracking Shot

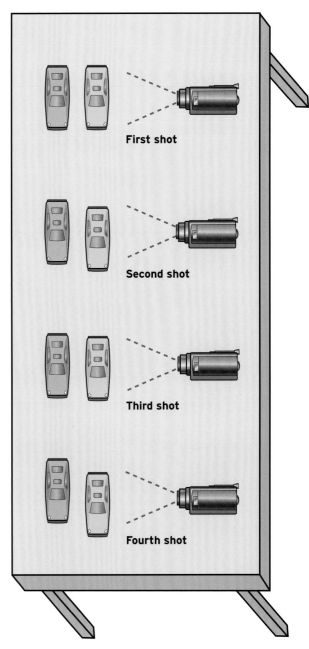

Line the cars up with the camera, and shoot.

First shot

Move the camera and the cars. Use the onion skin to make sure the camera lines up with the cars again. Shoot.

Second shot

Move the camera and the cars. Make sure the camera lines up with the cars again. Shoot.

Third shot

Move the camera and the cars. Make sure the camera lines up with the cars again. Shoot.

Fourth shot

The Nightmare Before Breakfast

SCRIPT: A short horror movie starring an evil spatula and a defenseless egg. A frying pan plays a supporting role.

INGREDIENTS: Egg, spatula, and frying pan.

DIFFICULTY LEVEL 1

Go watch it.
www.klutz.com/ani

Chase scenes like this one are great places to practice the basic animation technique (shoot, move, and repeat). But they're also good places to understand that the basics can be played in a million different ways. Here, for example, we've used sound effects and a couple of angle changes to make a spooky drama. With different sound effects and angles, you could make a lighthearted romance. (Well, you might have to change the ending a little...)

When hints are inserted early in the story that suggest how the ending will go, filmmakers call it foreshadowing. For example, the shots in which the stove turns itself on and the frying pan slides into place are foreshadowings of tough times ahead for the egg. Very handy for building suspense. Keep it in your bag of tricks.

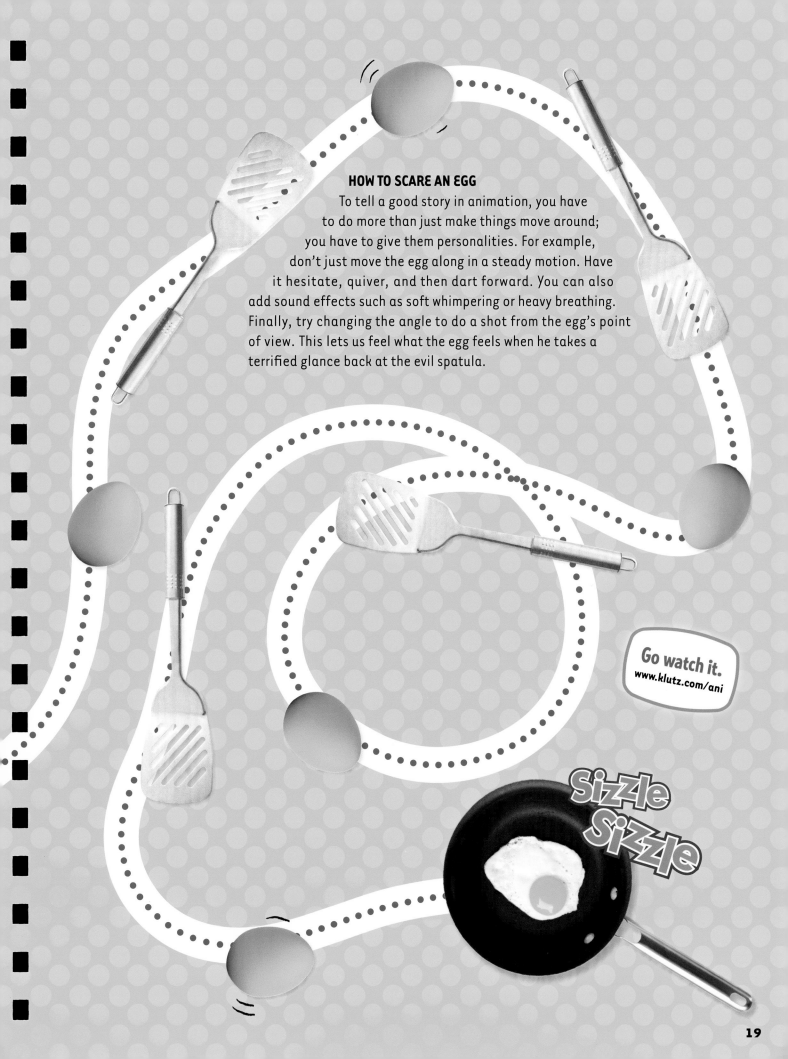

HOW TO SCARE AN EGG

To tell a good story in animation, you have to do more than just make things move around; you have to give them personalities. For example, don't just move the egg along in a steady motion. Have it hesitate, quiver, and then dart forward. You can also add sound effects such as soft whimpering or heavy breathing. Finally, try changing the angle to do a shot from the egg's point of view. This lets us feel what the egg feels when he takes a terrified glance back at the evil spatula.

Go watch it.
www.klutz.com/ani

Sizzle
Sizzle

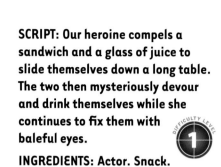

No-Handed Eating

Since the real star of our show is the sandwich, we shot low and put the sandwich in the foreground. You can choose a different angle (over the shoulder, from the side, or overhead) for a different feel and to tell the story a different way. As the plate slides down the table (shoot, move, and repeat) we asked our heroine to stay completely still so she didn't move while the plate did. Incidentally, the sliding sound effects and the big chomping sound are hugely important. Use them proud and loud.

How to Get a Sandwich to Eat Itself

Go watch it.
www.klutz.com/ani

1. Shoot the sandwich.

2. Take a bite.

CHOMP!

Sometimes you have to use a little imagination to record your sound effects. Try biting an apple instead of a sandwich to get a louder chomp. For the sliding sound, put a lot of weight on a plate and drag it across a counter. See page 13 for instructions on how to record and import homemade sound effects.

Here's the ghost of the last shot you took. The onion skin. Use it as a guide to locate the sandwich for the next shot.

3. Put the bitten sandwich exactly back into place. You can be exact, by the way, because the onion skin provides you the guide.

4. Repeat.

RUNAWAY CLAY

SCRIPT: A red blob crawls out from a container and proceeds to baffle and terrorize its human victim before finally returning to its home, mischief accomplished.

INGREDIENTS: Actor, clay.

DIFFICULTY LEVEL
1

Clay is an animator's best friend, especially when the animator is — like we are — a little drawing-challenged. With clay, anybody can make a great-looking blobby monster and with the magic of animation, anybody can make it come alive.

①
Clay emerges from yellow container.

②
Cut to close-up.

③
Preparing to swat.

④
Clay oozes up between fingers.

Go watch it.
www.klutz.com/ani

Claymation® is probably the second-most common kind of animation (after cartooning). All the Wallace and Gromit films are done with clay characters, and countless internet films use the technique as well. The preferred clay isn't the kind that comes out of the ground, by the way, it's plasticine, a formula originally developed more than one hundred years ago by an English art instructor. Plasticine doesn't dry out, doesn't flake, stain or melt in the sun. Most importantly, it shapes easily. Perfect for the job of animation. And, by the way, it's the formula we provide with this book. Obviously, you don't want to eat it, and go get your parents if you have any questions.

The clay may color your hands a little bit red, but it'll come off with soap and water.

5 Red blob attacks.

6 Red blob heads for cover.

7 Evades grasp.

8 Goes back home.

wink

To make your clay blob wink, flip over one of the googly eyes and draw a closed eye on the back. Add a ding sound effect.

CLAY HERO

SCRIPT: Our hero, The Blob Man, explores a desktop and has a series of office supply adventures.

INGREDIENTS: Actor. Random office supplies.

DIFFICULTY LEVEL 1

Check out the video online for our approach but don't worry about sticking to the script too closely. The reason we did it the way we did had mostly to do with the fact that we happened to have a stapler, paper clips, and a key on hand. If you only have a pair of scissors, a roll of tape, and a bent spoon, you should go with that and write a script accordingly.

To suspend him in the air, attach him to the wall using a pushpin.

Our hero bounces off stapler.

Our hero emerges from his bowl.

CLAY

He picks up a key and jams.

Cartoon Physics

Over the years animators have developed some tricks to make the physics of animation look better. Originally the goal was to get movements to look more realistic but animators quickly abandoned reality when they found that exaggerated reality was funnier. That's why when you watch Saturday morning cartoons you'll notice that things boing, squash, and stretch more energetically than they do in the real world.

Here are a couple of the tricks of the trade:

Go watch it.
www.klutz.com/ani

Squash and Stretch

When your character is bouncing or jumping along he should squash and stretch as shown to give an exaggerated sense of weight and momentum.

Ball in mid-air

Stretch in anticipation of impact

Squash on impact

Stretch as it takes off

Return to original shape in mid-air

Recoil

If your character is about to go from standing still to some energetic action like running, jumping, or throwing something, he should always first move away from his target before lunging forward. This helps prepare your audience for the motion to come and gives a sense of the force needed to lunge forward.

The recoil.   **The action!**

GOOGLY EYES

He lands in cup of googlies and finally gets some eyes.

PAPER CLIPS

Paper clips make nice skates. Record yourself scraping paper clips along the table to get the ice skating sound.

CLAYVOLUTION

SCRIPT: Red Blob shows off its multiple personality disorder. Enters changing room and morphs in front of our eyes into a fish. Goes back inside and turns into a lizard, monkey, dog, and something else that's hard to tell exactly.

DIFFICULTY LEVEL 1

INGREDIENTS: Clay, googly eyes, and a cup.

CHANGING ROOM

CHANGING ROOM

Go watch it.
www.klutz.com/ani

How to make a fish morph into a blob before your eyes

Place your fish in front of the camera and take a frame. Pick him up and mold him a little bit. Use onion skinning to put him back exactly where he was. Take a frame. Repeat until your fish is a blob.

Some Random Ideas for Other Clay Adventures

• ClayMan scoots around on can-opener skateboard. Has unfortunate accident in which head gets badly flattened. Learns to cope by wearing skateboard for a hat. The end.

• ClayMan meets pencil-top eraser; falls in love. Eraser spurns him. He makes wish and morphs into matching eraser shape and tries again. Happy ending.

• ClayMan explores kitchen sink faucet. Disappears, re-emerges in new pipe-like shape. Sells movie rights. The end.

• Two clay blobketeers engage in paper clip sword fight. One loses head but eventually finds it and puts it back on. Backward. Comic ending.

3

5

4

6

A STICKY NOTE TALE OF FECAL REVENGE

Duck, Duck, Poop

SCRIPT: Duck flies over man and very deliberately poops on his head. Man goes airborne in outhouse and gets payback.

INGREDIENTS: A bunch of yellow sticky notes and a black marker.

DIFFICULTY LEVEL **2**

SPLAT!

Go watch it.
www.klutz.com/ani

28

Get eight sticky notes and trace these ducks.

How to Make Your Bird Fly

1 On eight stickies, trace the eight ducks, conveniently numbered 1-8. See previous page.

2 Stick duck ① onto your background and shoot. Then pull it off.

3 Put duck ② where shown, and shoot. Repeat with ducks ③-⑧. Then go back to duck ① and do it all over again.

Trace the ducks.

Shoot the ducks in order, ①-⑧. Place them as shown.

How to Make Your Hero Wobble

| Original | Tracing #1 | Tracing #2 | Tracing #3 | Tracing #4 |

1 On a sticky note, draw a stick figure that looks sort of like ours. This becomes your original. Trace it three times.

2 Shoot the original and remove.

3 Put the first tracing in the same place. Shoot. Remove.

4 Repeat with the other tracings and cycle back to #1.

5 Since your tracings won't be exact, when you shoot them one after another the character will wobble a bit. A handy trick for adding personality.

How to Make the Outhouse Door Open and Close

1 Draw an outhouse that looks sort of like ours, with the door closed.

2 On three more stickies, trace your outhouse, but on each sticky, open the door bit by bit. See the examples.

3 Shoot the drawings in order ① ② ③ ④ to open the door. To close the door, shoot them ④ ③ ② ①.

The original

How to Make the Balloon Inflate
and the Outhouse Float Away

1 Draw a small balloon on a sticky note and stick this onto the top of the traced outhouse.

2 On another sticky note, draw a slightly larger balloon, and replace the smaller balloon.

3 Repeat two more times. Done.

4 To get the outhouse to float away, position them as shown and shoot them one at a time.

THE END

Lawn Skating

SCRIPT: Our star skates across the lawn, performs a dramatic routine, then finishes with a lovely face-plant and slide-off.

INGREDIENTS: Actor. A big empty lawn.

DIFFICULTY LEVEL **2**

When you make a real human being the star of your animation, you have a chance to make him or her do the impossible. In this case, that means skating across a lawn.

How to make the spin look real

Spin is faster with arms tucked in. Slower when arms are extended. Start upright and then spin into a crouch.

Go watch it.
www.klutz.com/ani

How to make the skating look real

1st shot

└ The back foot stays planted as you push off. The other foot moves forward.

2nd shot

Doesn't move.   Moves.

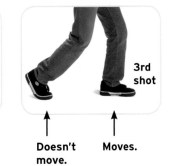

3rd shot

Doesn't move.   Moves.

4th shot

└ Now the back foot lifts, and you "coast" on the front foot.

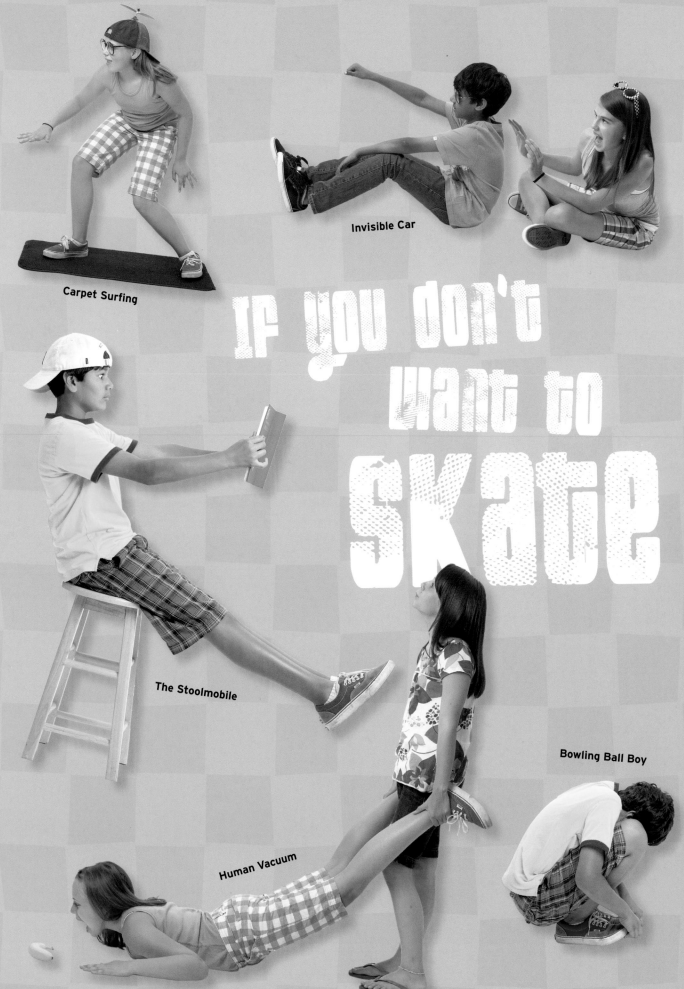

Carpet Surfing

Invisible Car

If you don't want to Skate

The Stoolmobile

Bowling Ball Boy

Human Vacuum

34

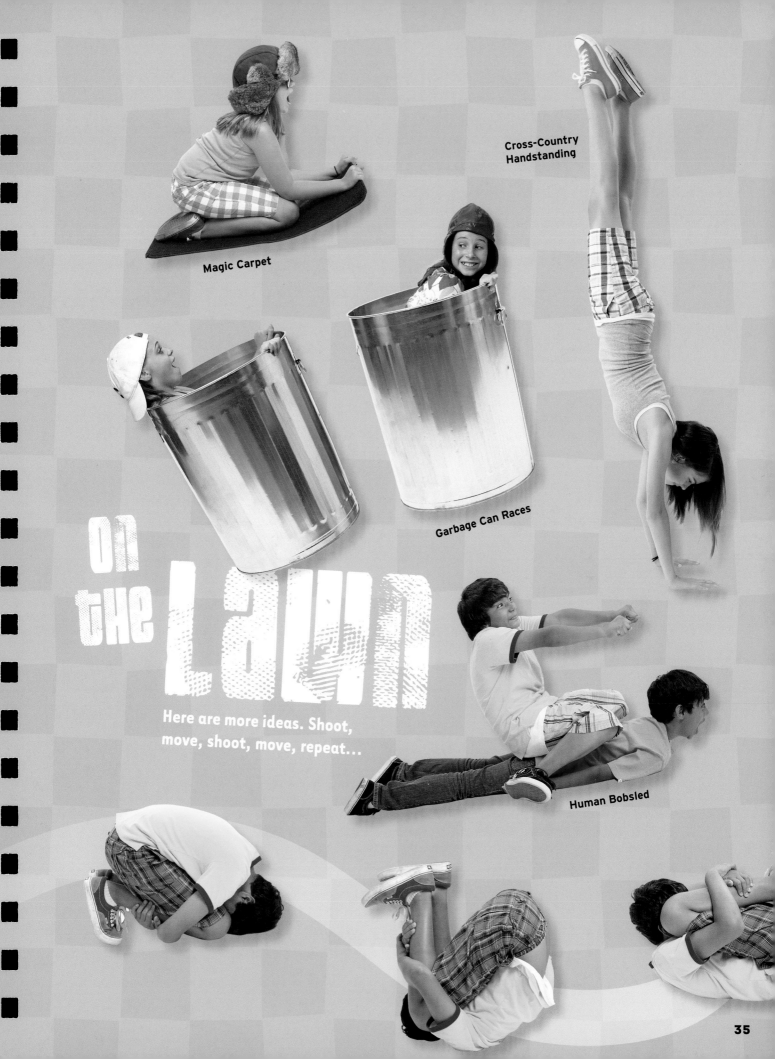

Magic Carpet

Cross-Country
Handstanding

Garbage Can Races

On the Lawn

Here are more ideas. Shoot,
move, shoot, move, repeat...

Human Bobsled

MAGIC ★ SHOES

SCRIPT: Man is enjoying a peaceful day in the park when he is approached by evil magic shoes. They drag him around, lift him off the ground, and then eventually drop him and steal the book.

INGREDIENTS: Actor. A big empty lawn. Shoes. Book.

Go watch it.
www.klutz.com/ani

1 **First scene.** The shoes approach and forcibly attach themselves to our hero's feet.

First shot   Second shot   Third shot, and so forth

2 **Second scene.** Make it look as if your hero is being dragged across the lawn by his shoes. Have him grab desperately at the grass. Shoot. Make him scoot backward. Shoot. Make him scoot backward. Shoot. Repeat.

First shot

3 **Third scene.** Our hero is still being dragged by his shoes, but this time they're pulling him into the air. This trick takes a little flexibility. Your hero has to kick his feet into the air, then you have to snap him at the highest point. It takes luck, practice, and timing. You can erase mistakes by selecting the frame where you got it wrong and hitting "delete."

Second shot

Third shot

Fourth shot

4 **Fourth scene.** Finally, our hero's shoes lift him off the ground and he flies. See next page for instructions!

HOW TO FLY

DIFFICULTY LEVEL 2

One of the most impressive low-cost pixilation effects is the flying man routine. Check out our online video for the basic look. An ordinary-looking guy, with his legs tucked underneath him, levitates and floats across a lawn. (See Magic Shoes.)

The trick takes timing, timing, timing. Your star has to jump and hit himself in the butt with his feet. And you, at the camera, have to catch the airborne moment, time after time. (The delete button is for the misses.)

The hoverboard

CLICK

Shoot.
Make your actor kick himself in the butt.
It'll give him more air.

CLICK

Shoot.

CLICK AND DELETE

Delete.
When you miss the moment, delete the frame and try again on the same spot.

Get ready to jump, and...

More Flying Poses

When you're ready to move beyond the basics, try taping a piece of cardboard to your superhero's feet and getting him to hop. Catch him with the camera mid-air. A hoverboard!

Or get him to do the "jump-and-hit-own-butt routine," but with the added prop of a broom. Makes a great witch. Or use an umbrella and get the Mary Poppins look.

To do the helicopter, jump in place with your arms out, rotating slightly with each jump.

The helicopter

Harry Poppins

The witch

Shoot.

Shoot.
If you don't move far between jumps, you'll look like you're hovering. Very cool.

Shoot.

Go watch it.
www.klutz.com/ani

PAPER DOLL
DISCO

SCRIPT: Two paper dolls boogie down.

INGREDIENTS: Paper doll punch-outs from the back of this book. Photos of you and your friends.

DIFFICULTY LEVEL
2

1 Punch out the paper dolls on pages 59–62.

2 Cut out photos of you and your friends' heads.

3 Put the paper dolls together using little pieces of clay to stick the joints together.

4 Lay your paper dolls on a tabletop with a cool background. It could be a photo or a drawing. Whatever you want. Make them dance. Paper dolls can move in ways that real people can't. Try to take advantage of this.

5 Use the SAM editing features to repeat dance moves and save time (See next page.)

KEY TRICK: Put your paper dolls on a table, not a wall. Shoot from directly above. <u>Much</u> easier.

Shoot down onto tabletop.

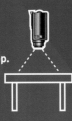

Go watch it.
www.klutz.com/ani

How to use the Editing Screen
to TURBO CHARGE your boogie

ADD SOUND

Go to the **sound tab** and click the **import sound button** and select your favorite tune.

10.0 fps

MAKE THEM DANCE TO THE BEAT

Adjust the **frames per second** to speed up or slow down the dance moves to match the beat.

REPEAT YOUR DANCE MOVE

Select all the frames in a movie by clicking on the first and last frame while holding down the shift key. Select **Duplicate** from the **Editing** menu at the top of the screen as many times as you like to keep your hero dancing.

Try making your dancers do impossible things (we made them trade heads).

famous FRUiT Speeches

SCRIPT: Classic speeches delivered by fresh fruit.

INGREDIENTS: Fruit, lip punch-outs (page 65), paper eyes (make your own).

DIFFICULTY LEVEL 2

Turn to page 65 and punch out the two sets of mouths you're going to be using for this trick. In each set, one mouth is wide open, one is closed, and one is midway. Your task will be to attach the lips to something that doesn't normally do much talking — we chose bananas and coconuts — and make them deliver some of the great speeches of all time. Check out the effect in the video online.

Go watch it.
www.klutz.com/ani

MY FELLOW AMERICANS...

How to Get a Banana to Talk

1 You have a choice about where to get your audio track. You can record your own speech or song using the computer's microphone and the recording function in SAM (see page 13). Or you can import a real song or speech that you have on your computer. The **import sound** function is under the **sound tab.** ▶

Import sound file

Record live sound

PRESIDENT OF THE UNIT

2 No matter where you got it, once you've imported your speech into SAM, it will show up on your timeline. The next step is to match up the different mouth positions with the speech. To do this, first play back your audio track a few times and pay attention to how the talking lines up with the squiggly line in your audio clip. Then attach the different mouth positions to your banana and shoot them, matching loud talking with the open mouth, other kinds of talking with the middle mouth, and silence with the closed mouth.

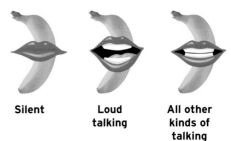

Silent   **Loud talking**   **All other kinds of talking**

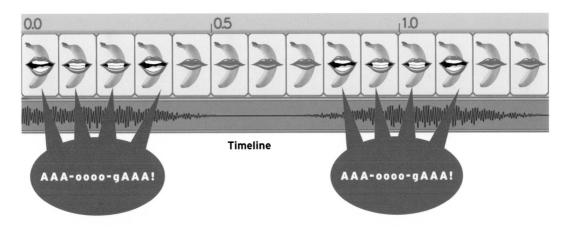

Timeline

AAA-oooo-gAAA!   AAA-oooo-gAAA!

Shortcut: Instead of shooting each mouth position multiple times, select Duplicate from the Editing menu at the top of the screen to duplicate the shots of each mouth position. Then drag them to the right place on the timeline.

3 The final step is to make minor adjustments by deleting a frame here and adding a frame there to get the speech and the mouth positions matched up precisely. The squiggly line on the audio clip is helpful for this step. Voila! Talking fruit.

I AM NOT A CUKE!

First shot **Second shot** **Third shot** **Etc.**

How to Make Nigel
TAKE A FALL

TAKE A WALK WITH NIGEL

DIFFICULTY LEVEL 1

1. Go to page 67 and punch out all eight of these guys. We call them Nigels 1–8.

2. Place ① where shown, and shoot.

3. Remove ① and place ② where shown, and shoot.

4. Repeat with ③ through ⑧. At the ninth shot, cycle back to Nigel ①. You can make him walk forever by just repeating the cycle. Pretty nifty.

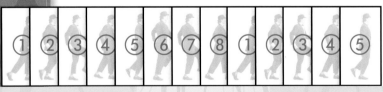

① ② ③ ④ ⑤ ⑥ ⑦ ⑧ ① ② ③ ④ ⑤

Waaahhhh!!

How to Make Nigel Fall from Book to Book

SCRIPT: Professor Nigel Plod walks in place on the cover of a book before leaving it and falling off the edge of a table into a series of other books which alter him in mysterious ways.

INGREDIENTS: Punchouts from page 67, some books (wrapped in paper with your own titles on them), a table.

Go watch it. www.klutz.com/ani

THE ADVENTURES OF NIGEL PLOD

HOW TO MAKE NIGEL WALK IN PLACE

Put Nigel ① on the cover of a book and shoot. Replace with Nigel ②. Shoot. Repeat with Nigels ③—⑧. To keep him walking, start all over again.

THE FRENCH REVOLUTION

HOW TO MAKE HIM LOSE HIS HEAD

Fold a piece of white paper and hook it over the top of the photo.

HOW TO MAKE HIM MULTIPLY

For this trick you need to put four Nigels into each shot. For the first shot, arrange as shown. For the second shot, replace number ④ with number ⑤, number ③ with number ④, number ② with number ③, and number ① with number ②. For the next shot, everyone continues to scoot down one spot. Repeat. A little parade of Nigels!

FUN WITH MULTIPLICATION

For shot number 2 replace this one with ②.

Replace this one with ③.

Replace this one with ④.

Replace this one with ⑤.

FLYING FOR THE HOPELESSLY EARTHBOUND

HOW TO MAKE THE BOOK FLY AWAY

Use fishing line.

? What other magical Nigel-transforming books can you think of?

spacehero

SCRIPT: Our hero flies through space battling aliens. After an epic battle with an evil hole punch, he crash lands on a planet and miraculously recovers.

INGREDIENTS: Take a picture of yourself with a cape on and cut it out, or you can cut a superhero out of a comic book. You'll also need construction paper, googly eyes, the space background on page 58, and a hole punch.

DIFFICULTY LEVEL
1

Boing!

Place the cut-out on the space background from page 58 (or some other background). Shoot, move, shoot, move, and repeat as always.

Make your hero punch out the space monsters and use the boing sound effect.

Make your own monsters by cutting them out of construction paper and attaching googly eyes with tape.

Go watch it.
www.klutz.com/ani

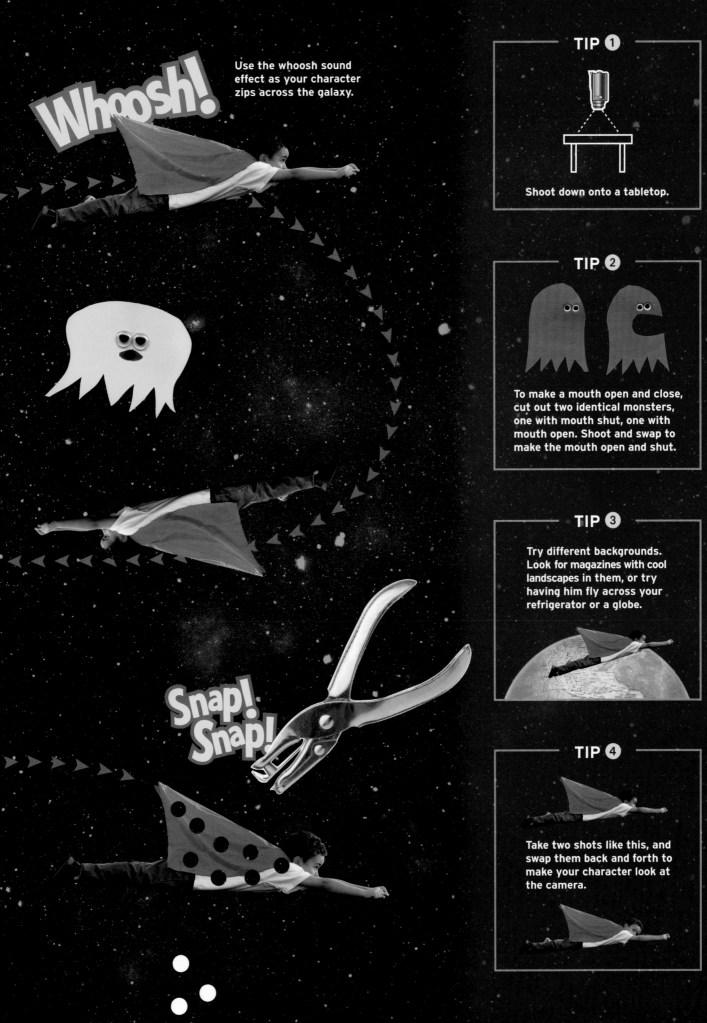

Whoosh!

Use the whoosh sound effect as your character zips across the galaxy.

Snap! Snap!

TIP 1

Shoot down onto a tabletop.

TIP 2

To make a mouth open and close, cut out two identical monsters, one with mouth shut, one with mouth open. Shoot and swap to make the mouth open and shut.

TIP 3

Try different backgrounds. Look for magazines with cool landscapes in them, or try having him fly across your refrigerator or a globe.

TIP 4

Take two shots like this, and swap them back and forth to make your character look at the camera.

Unmelting
ICE CREAM

SCRIPT: Plate full of sloppy white mess shapes itself into an ice cream sundae. Accompanied by orchestral score.

INGREDIENTS: Plate. Ice cream.

DIFFICULTY LEVEL
1

Time lapse photography allows you to see motion which would normally be too slow to notice. It's a kind of animation because it blurs a series of photographs into a moving image. But unlike other kinds of animation, all you have to do is set up the camera and walk away. Really easy. The trick is finding the right subject.

2:00

1:30

Here are a few other time lapse subjects you could try:

Busy street • Clouds • Your family at dinner • View out your window • Snails

Bread baking in the oven • Painting a picture • A fish tank

① TIME LAPSE

The time lapse screen

For this trick we used the ◄ time lapse tab in SAM.

We set it to take one frame every 30 seconds by putting the blue slider at 30s. Then we pushed the **time lapse button.** ▶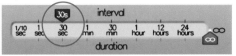

We moved the red slider to infinity. This means it will keep taking pictures until you tell it to stop.

② GOING BACKWARDS

First, select all the frames in the timeline by clicking Ctrl/A on a PC or Command/A on a Mac. Then select **Reverse Frames** from the **Editing** menu at the top of your screen to make the ice cream unmelt.

TA-DA!!

12:30   12:00

Go watch it.
www.klutz.com/ani

attack of the self-eating SAND SNAKE

SCRIPT: A snake chases its prey in a circle and ends up swallowing itself.

INGREDIENTS: A handful of dry sand. Piece of black construction paper. An old toothbrush can help.

DIFFICULTY LEVEL 1

1 Spread your sand out on a piece of black construction paper. Spread the sand evenly using the side of a pencil.

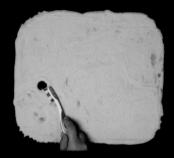

2 Use an old toothbrush or something like it to clear a little circle of sand. Shoot.

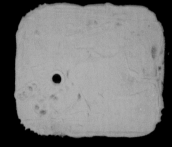

3 Erase your little circle and make a new one a little farther along. Shoot again.

CHOMP!

6 Have the snake lunge forward and close his jaws. He misses his prey the first couple of times.

7 The snake starts to eat himself!

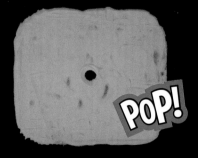

POP!

8 The snake swallows himself whole and disappears.

DON'T HAVE ANY SAND?
You can animate with anything you can scratch off. Fill a cookie tray with shaving cream and scratch a drawing. Or use…
• Flour
• Finger paints
• Chocolate syrup

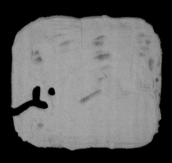

4 Using a toothbrush, clear out the sand to make the outline of a snake with his jaws wide open.

5 Make the snake chase the little dot around in a circle.

Go watch it.
www.klutz.com/ani

Whoosh! Pow!

IT'S ALL ABOUT THE SOUND EFFECTS
Pick a good chomping noise for your snake, a good popping noise for when he swallows himself up, and slide a penny around in the sand to make the sound of the crawling snake.

Difficult trick but one of our favorites. You have to know your way around the computer pretty well to do this. Keep your plans modest and try a simple version of the trick first.

Magical, Moving Family Photos

SCRIPT: Family photos come to life, steal each other's hats, make faces, start a fight.

INGREDIENTS: Picture frames, a tall stack of photos that you'll have to shoot and print.

1 Figure out what you want to happen in the picture frames and shoot it as video. Keep it simple and short. (Example: Girl waves, makes weird face, the end.)

import ↓ and share 🌐
buttons are up here.

2 Import the video into SAM by clicking the **import button** and selecting your video file. Then export it as a series of photos by going to the **file menu** at the top of your screen and selecting **export** and then **image sequence**.

20 seconds of video will give you 200 photos. That's about what we did, and that was plenty.

3 Print out all of the photos on your printer. (It's easier if you put them all in one document and then print the document.)

You'll need a lot of paper and a lot of ink.

Remember, this trick is tricky. You really need to know your way around your computer.

Go watch it.
www.klutz.com/ani

OUR WALL IS REALLY A FLOOR
Set up a scene on your floor that looks like a wall. We put books and a plant on their sides and shot down on them from above.

Take the top photo from your stack, and place it in the frame. Then take a picture.

Remove the photo and replace with the next one from your stack.

Then take a picture.

Do the same thing with the third picture...

...and the fourth...

...and so on. All the way through your stack. This will take a while, but it will be worth it. Check it out online.

FOUR OTHER
PHOTO ANIMATION IDEAS

TALK TO YOURSELF
Take a series of photos of yourself in action. Print them out and shoot them one by one in a picture frame.

MAKE NIGEL WALK DOWN YOUR ARM
Tape Nigel to your arm and shoot the pictures in sequence as shown on page 67.

CEREAL BOX MOVIE
Use photo animation to make the picture on your cereal box come to life.

THE MAGIC BOOK
Make a moving picture book by taping a series of photographs into the book and shooting them one at a time.

Rotoscoping means turning video into animation.
We did it by tracing pictures right off
our computer screen.

ROTOSCOPING

SCRIPT: Balls juggle themselves, then a juggler magically
appears... balls and juggler change in mysterious ways.
INGREDIENTS: Pen and paper, markers.

DIFFICULTY LEVEL
3

1 Shoot some video.
Choose something that
loops, like juggling,
jumping rope, or
running in place.

2 Import the
video onto
your computer.

3 Play the video back full screen
and pause it.

4 Put a piece of typing paper over your
screen and outline the video with a
felt-tip pen. (It's important to use a
soft pen so you don't damage your
screen; no ball points!)

5 Advance the video forward about
three frames and trace it again on
a new piece of paper.

6 Repeat steps 4 and 5 until you have
completed a loop. (I.e., your juggler
is right back where he started with
ball number 1 in his right hand.)

TIP 1: Import the original
sound from the video, and
line it up with your drawings
in SAM.

TIP 2: Don't worry about
getting the drawings too
precise. Messy drawings
give your rotoscope a
pleasant wobble.

7 Shoot your drawings in sequence in SAM
animation. Adjust the frames per second to get
the pacing to match the original video. If you
drew every third frame it should be about right.

8 After you've shot all of your drawings select
Duplicate from the **Edit** menu at the top of
your screen to loop what you've done.

TIP 3: Try photocopying or
tracing your drawings
and coloring them in
different ways to get
variations on your
original sketches.

Go watch it.
www.klutz.com/ani

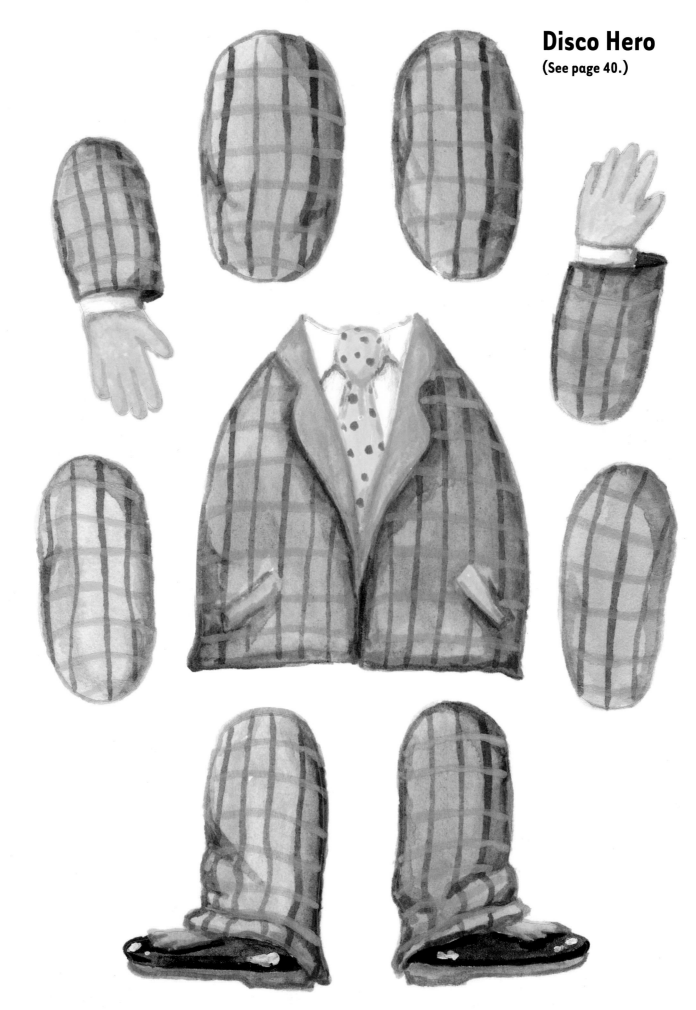

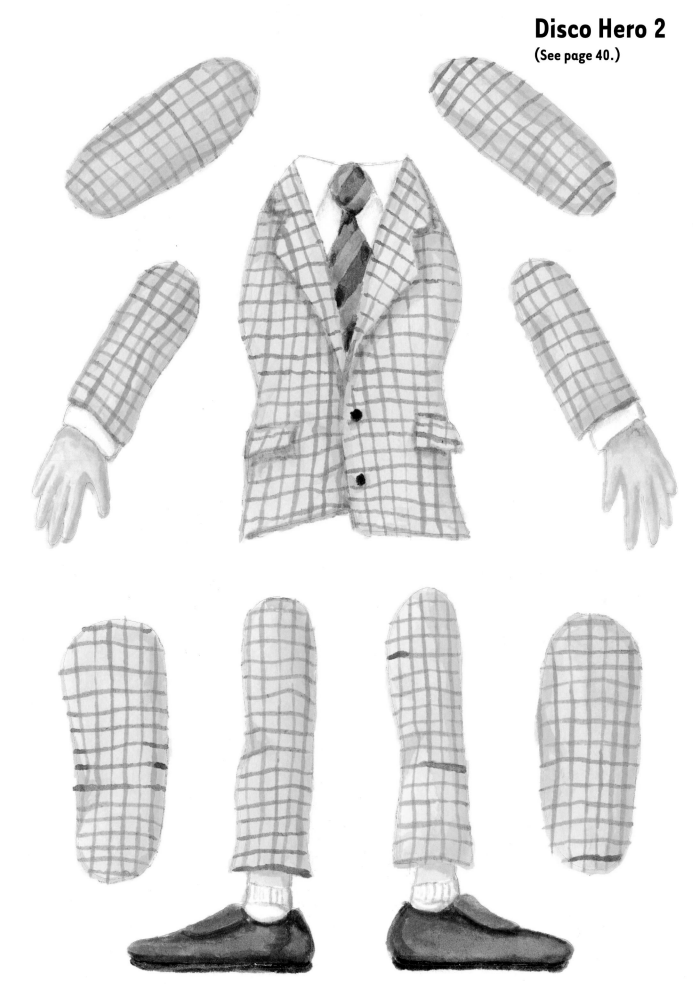

The Many Mouths
Punch-Out Page

(See page 42 for instructions.)

66

The Nigel Plod Punch-Out Page

(See page 44 for instructions.)

The Nigel Plod Punch-Out Page

(See page 44 for instructions.)

ACKNOWLEDGMENTS

Editors
John Cassidy &
Nicholas Berger

Animator
Nicholas Berger
(except for *The Nightmare
Before Breakfast*,
by Mike Attie)

Design
Kevin Plottner

Illustration
Buc Rogers
Liz Hutnick

Photography
Peter Fox
Nicholas Berger

Production
Patty Morris

Help
John Edmark

Brian Gravel, Chris Rogers
and the whole team at the
Tufts University Center for
Engineering Education
and Outreach

Craig Fry at Creativity, Inc.

David Malin

Inspiration
Preston Blair
Mike Jittlov
Caroline Leaf
Norman McLaren
George Méliès
Nick Park
Pes
Jan Svankmajer

Models
Tessa Barry, Laurel Fisher,
Ava M. Hallini, Marina Hallin,
Anand Josh, Sarah Limb,
Alexandra Livingston, Jordan
Parker, Arturo Montes, Bill Olson,
Ashvin Srinivasan, Avery Zenger

Credits
Plasticine Package: Nose ©
iStockphoto.com/Thomas_EyeDesign.
Page 2: Laptop © iStockphoto.com/
CostinT. Film background © iStock-
photo.com/BlackJack3D. Page 4:
Chair © iStockphoto.com/FeodorKo-
rolevsky. Phenakistoscope by David
Barker. Page 5: Egg © iStockphoto.
com/selensergen. Snail © iStockpho-
to.com/tomonikon. Page 7–8: Laptop
© iStockphoto.com/LDF. Page 7 & 10:
Camera © iStockphoto.com/PLAIN-
VIEW. Page 15: Wall background
© iStockphoto.com/ROMAOSLO.
Tape © iStockphoto.com/aurumarcus.
Pages 15–16: Car illustrations by
Buc Rogers. Page 17: Table illustration by Buc Rogers. Page 18: Oven
© iStockphoto.com/Petegar. Page
18–19: Egg © iStockphoto.com/
selensergen. Spatula © iStockphoto.
com/biosurf. Page 19: Frying pan
© iStockphoto.com/bluestocking.
Page 21: Teeth © iStockphoto.com/
Suzifoo. Page 23: Wallace & Gromit
© DreamWorks/Photofest. Page 28:
Sky background © iStockphoto.com/
DNY59. Duck © iStockphoto.com/
Chepko. Page 29–31: Pencil © iStock-
photo.com/NickS. Page 32: Squirrel
© iStockphoto.com/Tomacco. Pages
32–33: Grass © iStockphoto.com/
webphotographeer. Page 36:
Shoelace © iStockphoto.com/adisa.
Page 38–39: Background pattern
© iStockphoto.com/moorsky.

Page 40: Disco ball © iStockpho-
to.com/Kraska. Background
spotlights © iStockphoto.com/
deliormanli. Camera illustration by
Buc Rogers. Page 40–41: Dancing
Suits by Liz Hutnick. Need names of
Models. Page 42: Podium © iStock-
photo.com/GeofferyHolman. Star
banners © iStockphoto.com/angeal.
Presidential seal © Stan Nelsen -
Fotolia.com. Page 43: Cucumber
© iStockphoto.com/alex282. Page
44: Wood grain © iStockphoto.com/
CreativeArchetype. Page 45: Wallpaper
© iStockphoto.com/billnoll. Small book
© iStockphoto.com/fabphoto. Page
46 & 58: Outer space © iStockphoto.
com/sololos. Planet surface ©
iStockphoto.com/ZeeGee. Page 47:
Hole puncher © iStockphoto.com/
TokenPhoto. Globe © iStockphoto.
com/kemalbas. Page 48: Cherry ©
iStockphoto.com/MistikaS. Ice cream
scooper © iStockphoto.com/DNY59.
Clock © iStockphoto.com/Viorika.
Page 50: Hand © iStockphoto.com/
Briss. Page 51: Tray © iStockphoto.
com/Robinmaby. Shaving cream ©
iStockphoto.com/mantonis. Page 52:
Books © iStockphoto.com/redmal.
Page 53: Camera © iStockphoto.com/
jaroon. Laptop © iStockphoto.com/
Colonel. Printer © iStockphoto.com/
ambrits. Page 53–54: Paper stack ©
iStockphoto.com/Luso. Page 54: Paper
sheet © iStockphoto.com/2happy.
Page 55: Cereal box © iStockphoto.
com/redmonkey8. Page 59–62: Suit
illustrations by Liz Hutnick. Page 63:
Ratoscope by David Barker. Page 64:
Girl/mirror illustration by Buc Rogers.
Page 65–66: Lips by Liz Hutnick.
Page 66: Frame © iStockphoto.com/
gbrundin. Page 73: Curtain ©
iStockphoto.com/narvikk.

If you liked this book, you'll <u>love</u> Tricky Video...

...The Complete Guide to Making Movie Magic is a complete step-by-step set of instructions for creating low-tech versions of Hollywood special effects. Designed for the beginning filmmaker equipped with nothing trickier than the family video camera, **Tricky Video** shows how to sink a 90-foot basket, how to stage a good-looking punchout, how to play with gravity, how to get a banana to sing the blues, how to stretch your arm across the room, and 20 other similarly impossible effects.

All the tricks can be seen on-line (klutz.com/tv) and all the answers to all the how-did-they-do-that kinds of questions are in the book. It's a complete multimedia package ready to inspire and instruct the next generation of filmmakers.

Available at klutz.com or retailers everywhere.

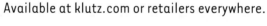